FINDING AND FOLLOWING THE PATH TO YOUR PASSION

The Power of Passion

FINDING AND FOLLOWING THE PATH TO YOUR PASSION

Renee Fowler Hornbuckle

Unless otherwise indicated, all Scriptures quotations are taken from the King James Version or the New International Version of the Bible

The Power of Passion: Finding and Following the Path to Your Passion
Copyright © 2002 by Renee Fowler Hornbuckle
Revised Version & Reprinted 2012
www.reneehornbuckle.org

Library of Congress Catalog – in Publication Data

ISBN 978-1480042056

Printed in the United States of America

Published by Jabez Books
(A Division of Clark's Consultant Group)
www.clarksconsultantgroup.com

All rights reserved. No part of this book may be reproduced, stored in a retrieval system, or transmitted in any form or by any means, electronic, mechanical photocopying, recording, or otherwise, without written consent of the publisher except in the case of brief quotations in critical articles or reviews.

    1. Success--Religious aspects--Christianity

Acknowledgements

I dedicate this book to my wonderful, distinguished, and amazing mother, Marion Virginia Fowler Armstrong, who has helped me to recognize my full potential. Your love and kind words encourage me to be ALL that God has called me to be. Thank you for believing in me!

To my three dynamic children: Matthew, Rachel, and Jordan, who share me with others! You have helped me to recognize the importance of living for Christ. May you always be empowered by the power of your passion as I train you in the things of the Lord! I love you!

And to the beautiful women and men around me who encourage me to continue in all that I do, and constantly remind me of what God has called me to do as I continually see their lives transformed through learning to love who they are. Your love and support is greatly appreciated and valued! Continue to love yourself!

Contents

Are You Ready To Succeed?

Chapters
1. What Is This Passion Thing?
2. What In The World Is My Passion?
3. Preparing For The Passionate Life
4. True Passion Requires A Positive Attitude
5. Prosperity And Passion
6. Ignite Your Passion
7. Live Your Passion

Conclusion: Final Thoughts

Are You Ready To Succeed?

In today's modern times, we are all encouraged to be successful and to succeed in life. Daily society's definition of success is constantly being hurled at us as women. For example, if we look at today's modern woman who lives by the expectations of being a superwomen...you see her as the one who preps in the mirror as she drives her expensive car to her corporate office after dropping her children off at school or at other activities, having cleaned her home and prepared the day's meals; she volunteers after work and gives back to the community - she's in command and in demand. She is every woman's envy; dressed in tailored suits and designer shoes she brings home a hefty paycheck that is spent on exotic trips, her pedigreed dog and all her designer wants. This 'modern woman', the one others envy is the same one I see every week in my office, or who inboxes me on FaceBook looking for answers about her life passion. The face is different, the personality also, but out of the mouth is the same desperate cry, 'How do I follow and purse MY passion?"

It is for these **_women (and men)_** that I write this book. I certainly understand the 'transition' experience. My personal life goal was to reach the top of the fortune 500 corporation at which I was employed. Steadily and quickly, I climbed that ladder of 'success' not realizing that I was destroying myself, neglecting my family and suffocating my purpose in the process. Sure, I was the 'envied' one, but I was definitely not the FULFILLED one!

The crazy thought came to me one day, 'What if you left and did what you really enjoyed?' My mind was in turmoil: what would it cost me? Don't misunderstand me, I was tough and believed I could handle anything, but could I deal with walking away from what I was trained and educated to be? Did I have the courage to abandon external pressures for internal peace? Finally in search of that internal peace I said, "Yes". I had to choose to embrace the "POWER OF MY PASSION."

In embracing that passion, the first season of transition involved becoming a full-time mother. And you talk about difficult! Everyone around me thought I was insane. They told me that I was throwing away my career, my life and all my education. But I knew that I was on the right path. The decision I made was not an easy one, but it was one I knew I had to make. So with a plan (you just can't walk away – you have to prepare); this was the beginning of me learning to do what I wanted to by following my passions and going after what I wanted. This transition ultimately landed me working in ministry, ultimately doing what I love to do!

Like me, you've probably said, "I am following my dreams." *Are you really*? Or, are you entangled in a web that you cannot get out of? Are you caught up with hefty incomes that allow you to have and maintain a certain lifestyle? Are you stuck in positions that really have less to do with your passions, but more to do with your comfort? Now that the economy has shifted, and many are faced with transitioning lifestyles; are you prepared to step into your passions?

A young lady, who I once mentored, put it like this:

> *"I was sitting at my desk mixing make-up colors and sketching eye-shadow applications, when I finally awakened to the fact that I enjoyed playing with make-up more than I enjoyed corporate America."*
>
> That young lady – armed with a plan, now is in Los Angeles with her own makeup line, school and successful business to the stars!

Another e-mail read:

> *Subject: Mentor Needed*
>
> *Hi, Pastor Renee,*
>
> *To get straight to the point, I desperately need a mentor and I would like for it to be you. I would like to retire from Corporate America within the next 3-5 years and need guidance on how to do so. I desire the assistance of someone who has walked this road before and successfully made the transition from a corporate job to making a living from her passion/calling. I need spiritual, mental and financial advice on how to make this shift. Among other things, I am sure that my mindset, ideas and habits will have to change, and that now is the time to begin to make these changes. Please advise...*

> "Help, I've given this company all these years, and now I feel it is time for me to do what I want to do! Everyone thinks I'm nuts because I'm so close to retirement. What I want to do people think is humanitarian and humanitarians don't make any money. I've lost my fire, what do I do?"

Here is a testimony from a POWER woman who took action and followed her passion.

> *It has always been a desire of mine to live for God. Even when my walk was questionable, my inner desire remained the same.*
>
> *Every direction of my life, when I look back, pointed to this day. I noticed a shift in my desires to move from the classroom to something better (I taught school for 12 years). There had to be more for me...this eventually led to me landing a job at Enserch Corporation.*
>
> *My life literally changed in 12 months. For the next 12 years, I worked in corporate training and was promoted to a director's level position in Human Resources. I flew all over the country, completed my second master's program and participated in some of the finest professional leadership development programs. I even met the First Lady of the United States and shook hands with former Governor Ann Richards.*
>
> *The summer of 2000, I realized something was happening to me again. I found it increasingly difficult to enjoy my job. What I loved, I was dreading. I was put on notice the latter part of August that the business unit where I managed a staff of seven people was being considered for*

downsizing, I felt so empty and alone. By December, we had one of the best Christmases ever. My son was a senior at Morehouse College, and my daughter was a sophomore at Clark in Atlanta, but I was just empty on the inside.

On January 5, 2001, the telephone rang. My manager said, "I need to talk to you today." My time had come again, another major shift in my personal life. I told my manager, the vice president and the president of the business unity I was thinking about leaving.

I decided to talk to someone who would understand what I was going through. Actually, I wanted someone other than the people with whom I worked to "talk" me into staying.

I made an appointment with Pastor Renee Hornbuckle. I had an opportunity to hear her personal testimony of leaving her corporate job to do the work of ministry. Pastor Renee greeted me with a warm smile as she sat in her beautifully decorated office with scented candles. I gave her a brief overview of my dilemma, carefully laying out each piece so that she could see that my heart was not ready to make this kind of step, which leads to uncertainty and public scrutiny from those we hold dear.

I will never forget the words she shared. She said, "Cathy, God is not satisfied with 99%. He wants our total commitment. All 100%. Now, weigh the pros and cons and see which is the better choice. Once you do that, then determine if God is speaking to you to follow you to follow your passion. If God is speaking, then you better obey, no matter what others are saying."

Now, this information was not what I expected. What I wanted was, "Get a plan, wait on God, and be clear."

It was through her candor and honesty, even though I was disappointed, that I knew she was giving me words from God.

I left Corporate America on March 16, 2001. It's been over a year now. I have cried, questioned and humbled myself, yet remained faithful.

I will always appreciate Pastor Renee for taking time with me that day. Her inspired words fueled me for the beginning of one of the greatest decisions of my life.

If you feel a pull from the Holy Spirit, don't fight it. Trust the Lord! Why? Because faith is the substance of things hoped for, the evidence of things not seen.

> *I did not see it, but I believed it. Thanks to Pastor Renee's step of faith to leave her corporate career for the work of the Lord, my desire to please God is being fulfilled.*
>
> *Elder Cathy W. Moffit*
> *Heartfelt International Ministries, Inc.*

Do any of these individuals sound like you? Then, I pray that this book helps you as much as it has helped "us". Notice I said, "us". Yes, I do follow my own wisdom.

My favorite book: The Bible tells us that God has an expected end for each of us. In Jeremiah 29:11, God says, "For I know the thoughts that I think toward you, saith LORD, thoughts of peace, and not of evil, to give you an expected end" (KJV). Think about what this verse says to you? It is my hope that through *The Power of Passion* that you will begin to see the expected end that awaits you!

We all must continually find out what we must do to follow our passions. I believe that if you apply the principles in this book that you will find yourself well on the way toward fulfilling your passions and achieving the great things that God has in store for you! I pray that you, too, will find nuggets of guidance that lead you to your passion!

Just be willing to evaluate where you are in life, then 'Find and Follow your Passion!'

Chapter 1

What Is This Passion Thing?

You Are Not What You Do

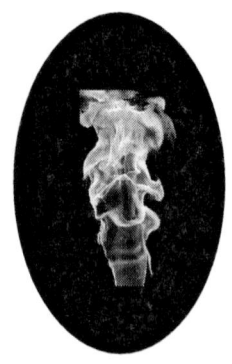

__Passion? What is it?__

Passion is an intense or strong desire. It is our deepest and most powerful emotion. God puts passion in each of us for two reasons. The first reason is that our passion will fuel our purpose on the earth. It is a driving force that energizes and encourages us to create and cultivate what we believe. The second reason God places passion in us is so that our passion will generate wealth. In our search for God, when we ultimately connect with Him, He will use the desires of our heart, the circumstances of our life, and His confirming word to secure and reveal our passions. Whenever you are passionate, you will be productive; when you are productive, you will be prosperous; when you are prosperous, you will provide for your purpose.

Fulfilling passion is what separates the "haves" from the "have-nots;" the "I have to try" people from the "maybe I'll give it a try" people. The separation occurs because we have not been challenged to find our own passions, to nurture that passion, and to make the most of our passion. Most of us have been taught, "We are what we do." What we do in life literally becomes who we think we are. I thought I was a corporate fast tracker, and when that was taken away, I didn't know who I really was. And boy, did I bottom out, until I got the revelation that I was not what I did. I was much more than that. What I did was not who I was. Nor was it what I became once I tapped into my passion.

> *What "I did" was not who I was. Nor was it what I became once I tapped into my passion.*

What do you mean? I'm glad you asked. See, we go through life being asked the question, "What are you going to be when you grow up?" It's like we have to have this all figured out, even if we are still discovering life. The better questions would be, "What is your dream? What excites you? What do you enjoy?" No one ever challenged us to pursue what we really enjoyed doing in life – they didn't ask, "What do you enjoy most in life?" As I was growing up, I enjoyed theatre and dance! I dreamed of being a great dancer and I loved acting! But during those times, there were not many of my culture represented on the movie screen or in the major dance companies. So given that I was smart; I was encouraged to pursue more of a definitive career. So as I enrolled and entered college, I enrolled in a major that would guarantee me employment versus what I loved to do. My parents meant well, but the thing I really wanted to do, I was discouraged toward doing. In fact, if most of us were honest, when we did say what we were passionate about, we were discouraged from pursuing it. Why? Maybe our parents or guardians didn't think we would be successful at pursuing our passions. Or maybe they didn't know how to set us on the path to pursuing our passions, so we could prosper. Maybe you were like Cathy or the other ladies you read about, they all had a lifelong dream yearning to be fulfilled, yet fears and other factors held them back and sent them in different directions. Regardless, I now know that God has a plan for your passion and wants you to be fulfilled in your passion. His plan includes prosperity, health, peace, joy and fulfillment of purpose.

- ❖ **Prosperity:** *3 John 1:2a – I wish above all things that you prosper. I pray that you may prosper in every way.* God has given everyone at least one ability to obtain wealth. That ability will be a part of your passion. When you work your passion, you will have the energy to keep going when you are tired. You will also have the persistence to forge ahead even when things go wrong. God had to put desire in you so that in spite of your situation, you would move on.

- ❖ **Health:** *3 John 1:2b AMP -- And (that your body) may keep well, even as (I know) your soul keeps well and prospers.* Be in good health. Exercise. Eat properly. Rest adequately. It is hard to enjoy prosperity in bad health. God's plan is for you to be healthy so that you can work your passion. When you operate in your passion, work related illnesses such as stress and anxiety will decrease.

- ❖ **Peace:** *2 Corinthians 13:11 NIV -- Finally, brothers, aim for perfection, listen to my appeal, be of one mind, live in peace. And the God of love and peace will be with you.* Do you have peace at your workplace even though it is chaotic? God promised to keep us in perfect peace. When you are living your passion you will have peace in the midst of storms around you. Even when you are working the process toward passion, you will be at peace until it is your time to move out in your passion.

- ❖ **Joy:** *Nehemiah 8:10 NIV -- For the joy of the LORD is your strength.* Joy is a by-product of passion. It causes you to energetically arise each day with an optimistic outlook on life. Do you enjoy what you do now, or do you dread getting up in the morning? If you do not feel the joy of the Lord in your workplace, you might assess if your lack of joy is due to you not being in your passion.

- ❖ **Fulfillment of Purpose:** *Jeremiah 29:11 -- For I know the plans I have for you, declares the LORD, plans to prosper you and not to harm you, plans to give you hope and a future.* Our purpose is fulfilled when we follow God's plan. The best way to fulfill your purpose is to find the passion that God has put in you. Ask Him to give you His plan for your passion. *Proverbs 19:21* says, "*Many are the plans in a man's heart, but it is the Lord's purpose that prevails.*" Whatever your passion may be it will only become prosperous if it is submitted to God. *Proverbs 16:3,* "Commit *to the LORD whatever you do, and your plans will succeed.*"

Planning A Passionate Life

God has a plan and you need a plan. He knows the plan even if you don't know what it is yet. Think about it. Even the best builders must first use a plan before they construct a home. Even though the master builder has an idea in his head what the house should look like, there are many details that must be considered. For example, plumbing, insulation and foundational strength are a few examples that must be well thought out. Without these details, the house would be destroyed under the slightest pressure. Planning is a tool that will make your life easier.

Planning is a logical systematic way of accomplishing a desired thing such as your passion. The first thing to consider is a timeline. When do you want your change? Sure, you can change now, but is it too expensive of a choice or will it take too much time? By that I mean, are you out of debt? Do you have a business plan? Have you spoken to anyone in the area of your passion that can give you sound advice? Have you done any research? Did you prepare and submit your resume into the new field that you are interested in? Have you counted the cost? Have you been honest with were you really are in life? So why did you really lose your job? Why did your spouse walk out? While there is no simple answer to these questions, you can still consult with God, receive His plan, make the adjustments in your life, and find hope. God's plans for us are not always the same as our plans. You may feel that you had the best job imaginable, but God knows that it is not what you were created for and He knows the right timing for all things.

When you are in pursuit of your life passions, there must be a balance. You have to consider what's required because you cannot allow others aspects of your life to suffer or to be neglected. For example, when my children where young, it was a season for me to pursue more passions that were home-based. When they were a bit older, I pursued a few more things, but when the school bell rang in the afternoon, I had to shift back to making certain I was pursuing the things that involved having a balanced home. You see, part of your plan involves judging the seasons of your life, and making the necessary adjustments. Read Proverbs, Chapter 16 when you get a chance, this will help you to better understand how GOD must direct our lives.

> *All the conditions will not be perfect for change, but if you do not prepare, opportunity will not come.*

All the conditions will not be perfect for change, but if you do not prepare, opportunity will not come.

Prepare and plan first; then watch your passion grow and flourish into reality. And always be mindful that in everything that you do that God has a great plan for your future.

Do you now understand passion?

Do you know what real passion is?

Do you understand what passion does?

Do you see why you must have a plan for your life?

Do you have a plan for your life?

Take some time alone and think on these things:

What is it that I desire to accomplish in life?

_____
_____
_____
_____
_____
_____
_____
_____
_____
_____
_____
_____
_____
_____
_____
_____
_____
_____
_____
_____
_____
_____
_____
_____
_____

If everything were absolutely perfect, I would:

Ask God to show you what it is that HE created you to do.

 Ask God to show you the assignment that HE created for you to do.

 Commit the passion of your heart to God in prayer!

Chapter 2

What in the World is My Passion?

Know What You Are Called To Do or You Will Do What Someone Else is Called To Do

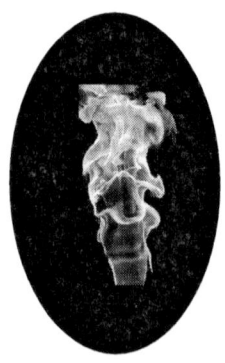

What in the world is My Passion?

Knowing your calling is where the journey begins. In order to move into your passion, you must know what it is. You must define your own empowerment according to the Word of God. The Word of God states that as believers we are given a position of dominion. When you understand this, then you can begin to define your calling. What is it that you are called to do? What is it that really bothers you? What problem have you seen that you feel compelled to come up with a solution to resolve? For me, I love helping others be empowered. So, what does that mean? It means that I don't take excuses or justification from people that want a better quality of life. I thrive off of helping others make the necessary change to bring about improved results in their life. It's not always an easy thing, but pastoring, coaching and guiding others to greatness are what I was born to do!!! It took some years for me to discover that, but like me, *you* must discover your own assignment. God has created something that only you can do. I find so many *aimless* people desiring to accomplish the assignment of other people. Then they become frustrated because they do not have the PASSION for that person's assignment, and as a result, there is no prosperity. Don't get caught up doing what others are called to do. Find what it is that God has assigned you to do.

Jesus was a good carpenter, but He was not called to just build things that carpenters build. Can you imagine if Jesus decided to join *Joseph and Sons Furniture Store*? We would have a lot of beautiful couches, but no Savior! Peter had a booming fishing business after he met Jesus. Although his business was blessed, he was called to be a fisher of men. Peter had to get in his purpose (which wasn't always easy for him if you read his life account in the Bible) to fulfill what God had for him. Moses turned out to be a good shepherd of sheep upon being sent to Midian.

> *As you identify your passion, God's purpose for you will be revealed.*

God was training him for shepherding people – to lead God's people out of bondage. Moses initially resisted God's call on his life to lead people. Had Moses stayed in the desert of Midian as opposed to going to Egypt to set God's people free, where would Christians who evolved from the Hebrew people be? God had a purpose for each of them and God has a purpose just for you. As you identify your passion, God's purpose for you will be revealed.

Seven Steps To Discovering Your Passion:

Step 1. List the top three things you do well.

_____
_____
_____
_____
_____
_____
_____
_____
_____
_____
_____

Step 2. List the top three things you love to do.

_____
_____
_____
_____
_____
_____
_____
_____
_____
_____
_____

Step 3. List three things your mentors, family and friends say you do well.

_____
_____
_____
_____
_____
_____
_____
_____
_____
_____

Step 4. List three things you could do the rest of your life without pay.

_____
_____
_____
_____
_____
_____
_____
_____
_____
_____
_____
_____

Step 5. List three things you do that energize you.

_____
_____
_____
_____
_____
_____
_____
_____
_____
_____

Step 6. List the thing(s) that show up on every list.

_____
_____
_____
_____
_____
_____
_____
_____
_____
_____

Step 7. If there is more than one thing, write the one that would best minister to others, solve problems or serve humanity.

_____
_____
_____
_____
_____
_____
_____
_____
_____
_____
_____
_____

If you honestly follow these steps, you will pinpoint your passion. It may take a little time, but do not get discouraged. Continue this exercise until you know that you have identified your passion. If you have a problem with this process, go through it with a mentor or a mature person that knows the real you. What you want to do is find a mentor or coach to help you identify your passion. If you follow these steps, your true passion will show up on every list. God will give you a passion that will minister to others, solve problems, or serve humanity. In return, the world will pay you for your personal services.

Walk In Your Highest Calling

Most people will likely have several items on their list. The majority of people spend 80% of their time doing things that will not bring them wealth. If you do a self-check, you spend 20% of your time doing things that are on your passion checklist. Do not fret. Some of the greatest people in the Bible spent years doing other things before the manifestation of their purpose. David was anointed king, but he went back to watching over sheep until God was ready for him. Paul stepped out too quickly, and had to go away to spend time in training before his purpose was clear. Joseph was even sent to prison before he walked in his purpose as the first in command under Pharaoh.

If you know your passion and you are not walking in your highest calling here is *what you do* while you *wait* for it to come into realization.

1. **Acquire information about your passion.** It only cost time to get knowledge. Make use of the library, bookstores and internet research. *Hosea 4:6, "My people are destroyed from lack of knowledge."* Knowledge is power!

2. **Take advantage of the experience you are gaining presently.** Even if you flip hamburgers for McDonalds, there is a business system that they use which causes them to be the greatest franchise in America. Study systems and see what you must learn to do before you move into your assignment.

3. **Find a mentor!** A mentor will help you get to where you want to go faster and with fewer mistakes. *Proverbs 13:10, "Pride only breeds quarrels, but wisdom is found in those who take advice."* Develop your master-mind group. Choose people who are already where you desire to go (spiritually, physically, and financially). Make sure they will hold you accountable to the advice given.

4. **Stay focused.** Do not get caught up in unnecessary things. Everything good is not God. Broken focus will keep you from your passion. Focus! Focus! Focus!

5. **Take at least 30 minutes a day to meditate and think.** This is an exercise that I have integrated into my daily life. It's during this time of meditation that I find that God gives me creative ideas!

6. **Finally, dream and journal!** It does not cost you a thing to have dream days where you reflect on the desires of your heart and your passion. Write down what God reveals to you in your journal as you dream, so that you can reflect on all the things that God will show you as you walk through your time of preparation.

My Personal Passion Agreement

List any specifics that you believe will help you in the pursuit of your passion:

_____
_____
_____
_____
_____
_____
_____
_____
_____
_____
_____
_____
_____
_____
_____
_____
_____
_____
_____
_____
_____
_____
_____
_____

To pursue my passion, I will commit to following the above steps for the next six months:

_____
Signed   Date

Chapter

3

Preparing for the Passionate Life

I enjoy what I do and guess what? I get paid for it! ~Oprah Winfrey~

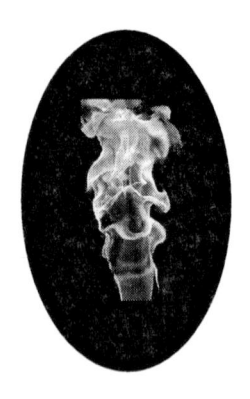

Preparing for the Passionate Life

Most people dislike preparation. Preparation is what you do in anticipation of a season that does not yet exist. It is crucial to your being ready to move into your season when the opportunity arises. Most people miss opportunities because in their season of preparation they are not focused on what is yet to come.

I know this well, because when I left Corporate America years ago to come home to what I thought was my passion (rearing my children fulltime), I was totally unprepared. Being a full time homemaker appeared to be easy, yet, it was the most difficult job

I ever had! Why? Because I had not properly prepared to be a fulltime mother. Don't get me wrong, I could cook and clean, but raise children fulltime, I was not fully prepared. I thought I could treat my children like staff, and I thought they would do as I commanded the first time. Guess what? I had a rude awakening. Of course, I succeeded, but what did I learn? I learned a valuable life lesson - make certain to always be prepared for whatever the next season of my life entailed.

The majority of my preparation had to do with my learning to love God and myself first. Once I was able to receive and practice this principle, then I could give to everyone else and properly plan to pursue future passions. Each time the seasons of my life changed, I was prepared. As I transitioned later from being home fulltime, adding ministry fulltime to the equation – I was up for the challenge, but again not before preparing first. I helped my then husband, served alongside him in ministry, and helped him push the cart up the hill. As I helped him build the ministry, once we achieved a

> *I strongly believe that because I've always believed in helping others succeed, that God has always strategically placed me into my passions and dreams.*

certain level, I began to coast into my own distinct personal ministry. I believe I was able to step into my own ministry because I had prepared. I now had the awareness that with each changing season I was required to prepare.

I strongly believe that because I've always believed in helping others succeed, that God has always strategically placed me into my passions and dreams. Let me pause here to introduce you to another powerful principle: **what you make happen for someone else, God will make happen for you!** In other words, when you help someone else pursue their passion, you will wake up and be in your passion. Why introduce this principle now -- because this principle is an important part of your season of preparation?

I recently watched a movie that dealt with a naval officer who was trapped in enemy territory. Before being trapped in enemy territory, he decided that he needed to leave the navy because for eight years He had only been studying, training and doing drills, and there was 'no war, no action'. In other words, why prepare for *nothing*? This lack of activity was draining his passion because he did not realize that preparation is vital for success.

Anyway, he got his chance to be in a real war. It was only then that he finally realized how important his preparation was. Everything he dreamed of and had prepared for was now happening – it was his moment – live or die, sink or swim, fail or succeed, be a team player or perish. All of these possibilities laid in the strength of his preparation. He was prepared for his passion! He was prepared for his big moment! It is the same for you and me. Do we just dream about 'one day' or are we making that 'one day' begin today through study, training and drills?

> *Do we just dream about 'one day' or are we making that 'one day' begin today through study, training and drills?*

Og Magdino was once quoted as saying, *"The victory of success is half won when one gains the habit of setting goals and achieving them. Even the most tedious chore will become endurable as you parade through each day convinced that every task, no matter how menial or boring, brings you closer to fulfilling your dreams."*

Prepare For Your Passion by Establishing The Vision For Your Passion

The first step is to create a vision for your passion. Vision is foresight or the ability to anticipate and make provision for future events. The vision statement for your passion should be what you want your passion to accomplish in the future. Vision is what leads you. The vision must be bigger than you, meaning that it reaches beyond you, and if it is not, then your vision is not a vision but a goal.

Vision gives your passion direction. It should be inspirational as well as sincere. Vision will provide you with motivation, an image, a tone, and a philosophy to guide you. Vision comes from deep within. For example, I know one of my callings or assignments in life is *to empower women in their purpose through equipping them with practical tools so they can enjoy an improved quality of life that is passion and purpose directed. To see women of all ethnicities, denominations and cultures transformed through "Women of Influence Inc.," which is the platform given to me by God to be able to take my ability (passion) around the world.*

My vision adds value to others lives, and is much bigger than me. In fact, my vision will take money and is outside of my geographical area. I will need access to transportation, several staff members, centers in different nations, etc. It is bigger than what I currently have and I have to trust God to get it done.

Some facts about Vision:

1. Vision doesn't just happen overnight – it is a process.
2. Vision is easy to lose, but hard to regain.
3. Vision is absolutely necessary for survival.
4. Visions have to be written.
5. Vision clarifies destination, without it you are lost.
6. Vision is God's way of getting you to think like Him – BIG!
7. Vision is within YOU – go find it.
8. Vision never becomes a reality without action.
9. True vision becomes a part of who we are.
10. Where there is vision, there is provision.

Prepare for Your Vision by Visualizing Your Vision

I love this scripture, *Habakkuk 2:2 KJV*, "And the LORD answered me, and said, Write the vision, and make [it] plain upon tables, that he may run that readeth it."

I really like Habakkuk 2:2-3 in The Contemporary English Version (CEV), ***"Then the LORD told me: "I will give you my message in the form of a vision. Write it clearly enough to be read at a glance. At the time I have decided, my words will come true. You can trust what I say about the future. It may take a long time, but keep on waiting— it will happen!"***

The next step is for you to visualize your vision. A mental image of your vision must be formed. Models such as vision boards, purpose cards and goal books will assist in the visualization process. Jesus always used stories to paint a mental image for the people. Paul compared the Christian walk to athletic competition. This process will amplify your thinking. It will help you instruct your inner spirit to bring your vision into fruition. A vision without action is just a dream.

Simply find a place to post the things that you envision. I like to use a beautifully framed board, and I post sayings, and pictures of what I desire to accomplish. Over the years, as I've looked at what I put on my vision board, prayed over it and begin to put a strategy in place, I can say that I've seen at least 90% of it come true! You must cherish and protect your vision.

> *"Cherish your visions and your dreams as they are the children of your soul; the blueprints of your ultimate achievements."*
> ~Napoleon Hill

So, God will give you the plan. It will be clear, write it down, so you can read it and refine it. And wait for the right time – prepare, get ready… because it will happen! Trust GOD that HE will make your dreams come true!

Prepare for Your Passion by Establishing a Mission Statement

Lastly, you must add purpose to your passion by making it your mission. A Mission Statement is a specific task with which a person is charged. It expresses your unique purpose for living. Most people cannot adapt to change because they are not clear about what it is that they are called to do.

When you are focused on your purpose, you will be able to adjust to any circumstance in order to fulfill your mission. Lack of focus is the number one reason why people do not get what they want. People who focus, prosper; those who do not focus struggle. Do you know what you want? Is your mission clear and simple? Do you know your BEST QUALITY? Your mission will only be successful if you are clear in what you feel you are supposed to do, what you are called to and what you care about. You will not be able to accomplish your plan unless you know what is required of you.

> *The vision that God gives to each of us is bigger than ourselves and will always affect more people than just ourselves.*

Your mission statement will have summary action strategies that will help you bring forth your vision. Your mission statement should be highly descriptive and cover a range of strategies and objectives while focusing on your top priorities – helping you to become clear on who you are. When you write your mission statement, answer the question, 'What do I desire to accomplish?' Once you clarify that, you must simply do it.

Jesus knew the urgency of completing His mission. *John 17:4 NIV, I have brought you glory on earth by completing the work you gave me to do.* He had to complete His mission in order for the Father to be glorified. Only through the completion of the mission could the Father be glorified. When you fulfill your mission on the earth, you bring glory to your Heavenly Father. Moses completed his mission by leading the Israelites out of bondage. Despite all the people problems Moses had, he blessed every tribe and died in peace. Since his vision was bigger than himself, he was able to lay hands on Joshua to succeed him before he died. Joshua went on to accomplish the purpose God had for His chosen people. The vision that God gives to each of us is bigger than ourselves and will always affect more people than just ourselves.

Steps to Proper Preparation!

I commit to the following emPOWERment Life Keys:

1. **I will take time with God and inquire of HIM.**
2. **I will seek HIM for strategy.**
3. **I will wait on the plan, and write it down. Habbakuk 2:2**
4. **I will develop a Dream Journal and Dream Board**

    ❖ Habakkuk 2:2-3, "Record the vision and inscribe it on tablets, That the one who reads it may run. For the vision is yet for the appointed time; It hastens toward the goal, and it will not fail. Though it tarries, wait for it; For it will certainly come, it will not delay." NAS

    ❖ Post Dream or Faith Pictures, Words and Photos. In Genesis 15:1-5, God gave Abraham a faith photo that would provide divine direction for his life. Gen 15:5, "Look up at the heavens and count the stars--if indeed you can count them." Then he said to him, "So shall your offspring be." NIV

    ❖ Get God's vision for your life, record it, pray over it daily, act on it, and watch it become a reality!

5. **I will develop My Vision Passion Statement: (Write it down)**

   VISION: What is your passion? What happens when you are giving your greatest gift to the world? How are people different as a consequence of having been in your presence? See it as an image. Use present tense. Answer these questions:

   - What gives you a sense of aliveness that feels "just right"?

   - What do you dream about?

   - What are blessings you could give back to the world?

   - Whose work or life inspires you?

   - What would you talk about if given an hour of prime time TV to influence the nation or the world?

   - What makes you angry enough to correct in the world?

   - What contribution of yours will be more profound than others doing something similar?

6. **I will develop My Mission Passion Statement: (Write it down)**

    MISSION: What about you (attributes, experience, skills, knowledge, passion) makes your vision possible? Who is your Self?

    - What are you an EXPERT in?
    - What is a true expression of who you are?
    - This will also impact your branding; your uniqueness.

7. **I will set achievable goals.**

    STRATEGIES/GOALS/PARAMETERS: How will you carry out your mission and vision? You start with a DRAFT PLAN! Have you ever had to write a paper? You start by drafting it out, and it takes time to get to the end result. Why now, do we want the end result before we go through the process?

    Process is necessary! The Bible references often, "in the process of time"... meaning that there are some things that are going to require a process (procedure, a practice, progression, method, course of action, method) involving time.

- **So scope out the big picture** - Write a general summary of what you want to accomplish with objectives, budget, time, assumptions, definitions, potential risks and issues that may arise and tie it to a goal. Make sure you write the pros and cons so you know where to focus downstream.

- **Clarify your goal.** Can you get a visual picture of the expected outcome? How can you see if you have reached your destination? **What strategies will accomplish your vision? Identify 4-5 goals within each strategy.** What make your goal measurable? What constraints do you have, like the limits on time, money, or other resources? **What internal and external forces surround each goal--those that encourage and those that may discourage your vision?**

"A good goal is like a strenuous exercise-it makes you stretch" - **Mary Kay Ash**

- **Write a list of actions.** Write down all actions you may need to take to achieve your goal. At this step focus on generating and writing as many different options and ideas as possible.

    - ✓ **What first steps can you take to accomplish your vision?**

    - ✓ **How can you increase encouraging forces, both internal and external?**

    - ✓ **How can you overcome internal/external discouraging forces?**

    - ✓ **Take a sheet of paper and write more and more ideas, just as they come to your mind. While you are doing this, try not to judge or analyze.**

- **Break into smaller tasks** - More specifically, assign tasks to yourself or team members, pieces of the project that will support how you will achieve your goal. In this assignment make sure to think proactively about the timeline and deadlines of the overall project in terms of allocating resources.

- **Analyze, prioritize, and prune** - Look at your list of actions. What are the absolutely necessary and effective steps to achieve your goal? Mark them somehow.

- **Create a list of action steps** - For each task, there should be a list of to-dos ranked in sequential order. Make sure this list can be changed, re-ordered and deleted if there are redundancies. After that, what action items can be dropped from in the plan without significant consequences of the outcome? Cross them out.

- **Prioritize** - Some steps are more important than others and some can be delegated to friends or co-workers. Based on days to deadline, task and action step importance, and number of steps remaining, create a master list of the top steps to do TODAY.

- **Organize your list into a plan.** Decide on the order of your action steps. Start from looking at your marked key actions. For each action, what other steps should be completed before that action? Rearrange your actions and ideas into a sequence of ordered action steps. Finally, look at your plan once again. Are there any ways to simplify it even more?

- **Monitor the execution of your plan and review the plan regularly.** How much have you progressed towards your goal by now? What new information have you gotten? Use this information to further adjust and optimize your plan.

When you properly prepare by effective planning, you will...

- Immediately grow in confidence.
- Have clear, focused, practical steps to follow.
- Save your most precious resource - time.
- Feel tremendous motivation and enthusiasm.
- Save money. Potentially lots of it.
- Create even better concrete results.
- Cherish each new day and its challenges.

PERSONAL CHALLENGE

Do you know what you want?

What is your vision?

Is your mission clear and simple?

Do you know your BEST QUALITY?

Who are you holding back by not completing your mission in life?

My Vision Statement
(Meditate, dream, and write what could be the end result of what you will have done in your life.)

My Mission Statement
(Define the action strategies that you will do that will help bring forth the vision. For example: My mission is to empower, motivate, and encourage others in the pursuit of their destiny.)

Chapter 4

True Passion Requires A Positive Attitude

If you do not believe in you,
no one else will

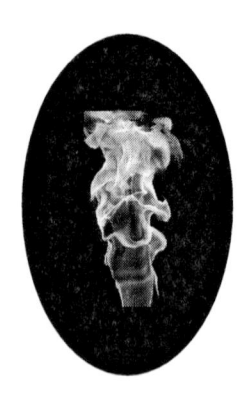

No Stinking Thinking

Do you really want to be in your passion? God is waiting for you to take the first step. Moses had a passion to see his people free. That is why he killed the Egyptian who was beating the Hebrew. But Moses did not believe he was the one to deliver his people. In fact, Moses gave God several excuses when God gave him his mission. Moses had to trust and obey what God was speaking to him. God told Moses to go, and He would teach him what to say. By faith Moses lived his passion and achieved his mission through obedience to God. When Moses came to the Red Sea all he did was stretch out his hands, God did the rest. Do you have enough faith in your passion to take the first step and let God do the rest?

Retrain Your Brain!!!!

Romans 12:2, "Do not conform any longer to the pattern of this world, but be transformed by the renewing of your mind. Then you will be able to test and approve what God's will is--his good, pleasing and perfect will."

The world has convinced many people that they cannot make it without its system. However, you cannot think like the world. You must get the mind of God. His mind will give you the confidence to work His plan for your life. *Luke 1:37 AMP, "For with God nothing is ever impossible and no word from God shall be without power or impossible of fulfillment."* You need God-confidence to protect you from the darts of negativity. Without His mind, fear and worry will take control. *2 Timothy 1:7 KJV, "For God hath not given us the spirit of fear; but of power, and of love, and of a sound mind."* The more you read God's Word, the more you will think like Him. Your

> *If you desire to truly follow your passions, then having a positive mindset is essential!*

faith will increase knowing that God has given you the POWER to fulfill His purpose for you on this earth.

Your life can change, literally overnight, by changing ow you think! How you think is a choice, and you can shift from negative thinking to positive thinking simply by choosing to change. If you desire to truly follow your passions, then having a positive mindset is essential! You must learn to think for yourself according to God and not buy into what the world wants to offer you.

Gideon is an example of one who bought into the world system. Gideon was commissioned to lead an army to victory for God. Gideon had a plan. He followed the plan of every great general and king and warrior before him, which was, more men, better the army will be. God changed Gideon's plan, but Gideon did not believe in himself. And even as God guided him, Gideon constantly questioned and doubted God. Gideon is known by many as a coward. Initially he was, but when he retrained his brain, he became one of the greatest warriors for God.

True Passion Requires a Positive Attitude

Seeds of doubt either lay dormant or are active in all of us. In order to accomplish what God has in store for us, we have to weed out those "doubt seeds."

Moses doubted his ability to be the great leader that he became. He looked at his past, his background, his circumstances, and his present and decided that he was not the person for the job. Yet, God had another plan. God used Moses in spite of Moses, as soon as Moses relinquished his fears and doubts and submitted himself to God.

Martin Luther King, Jr. was another person who yielded himself to the will of the Father. He did not believe that he was chosen to lead the Civil Rights Movement. He simply knew that he had a passion to change things from the way that they were. When fear and doubt followed him, and they did follow him, he yielded not to them. He had a positive attitude despite what *was*.

When everyone else doubted Dr. King, he learned to believe in himself and believe that he was the person for the job. All Americans have Dr. King to thank for the racial equality that is present in today's society. Dr. King believed in his passion.

Retrain Your Brain

Developing the right mindset may seem impossible to you right now, but you can do it. You do not have to stay the way you are! Build a positive mindset by working with positive affirmations (positive self-talk) such as "I love myself. I expect the best! I believe that I can!" Create several positive messages about yourself and your life, and write them down each day. Several times a day, read the affirmations aloud. The more you write and read them, the more you reinforce the positive messages in your subconscious mind. If you believe you can, you can!

> *The right attitude is also crucial because it is directly tied to how you act or behave.*

The right attitude is also crucial because it is directly tied to how you act or behave. If you think negatively, you will act negatively. If you think positively, you will act positively. In other words, if you believe you can, you will go out and take the necessary action to get it done!! You have to retain your brain!

Your positive attitude and enthusiasm will fuel your desires and the desires of others around you. The quality of your life will be determined by your attitude. Your attitude is determined by your thought. Your thought comes from your brain. "Retrain you brain" so that your positive attitude will cause you to live your passions!

What pressing thing do you desire to see changed or done differently? What hinders you from being a catalyst for that change? Are you allowing fear and doubt to hinder the passion that you have? Are you looking at your circumstances and situations? Your past and your failures? Do you doubt what you are called to do because you are controlled by fear or doubt?

List the thing(s) that you feel compelled to do.

_____
_____
_____
_____
_____
_____
_____
_____

List the hindrances that block you from doing that thing.

_____
_____
_____
_____
_____
_____
_____
_____

What will you commit to change in order to fulfill your passion?

_____
_____
_____
_____
_____
_____
_____
_____

Chapter 5

Prosperity and Passion

Passion without Prosperity is Impossible.

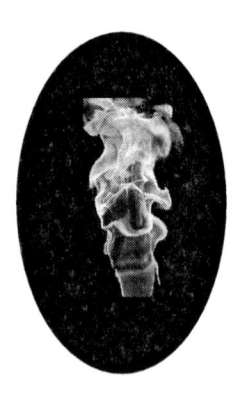

Personal Prosperity

Luke 16:10 NIV "Whoever can be trusted with very little can also be trusted with much, and whoever is dishonest with very little will also be dishonest with much.

*I*n order to turn your passion into prosperity, you must manage what you have now. If you mismanage your personal funds, you will do the same with your business or any future personal wealth. When you bounce a personal check, the consequences do not appear to be great, but they still affect your ability to walk in your prosperity. Mismanagement of personal or business funds can lead to lack, bankruptcy and lawsuits, which directly affects your level of prosperity. The lesson we must learn is that we must prove to God that we can handle the small things first.

If you want God to prosper your passion, here are some personal financial management actions you must take:

1. Put God first by giving your tithe.
2. Participate in freewill and charitable offerings or donations.
3. Develop and maintain a realistic working budget.
4. Eliminate wasteful spending.
5. Put a debt reduction plan in place.
6. Save for your passion.
7. Serve in the area of your passion.
8. Sow financial seeds into good ground by faith.

Your Passion will Cost You Something

"Suppose one of you wants to build a tower. Will he not first sit down and estimate the cost to see if he has enough money to complete it?" (Luke 14:28 NIV)

It is very easy to jump into a deal without looking at the details. Developing a financial plan for your passion will save you from disappointments. It is not wise to quit your job without knowing how provisions will be made for your necessities. This is the biggest mistake that I see people make. They get excited about their passion and jump into it feet first without looking at the process of preparation that they must go through and without counting the cost. At one time the Apostle Paul worked as a tentmaker when he was not passionately preaching the gospel. It may be for this season that you cannot work your passion full-time, but put together a three to five year strategy so when your season comes you will be ready. Your passion will cost you time, thought and

> *When you have your vision and mission clearly defined you will gain support for your passion.*

trials. *Proverbs 21:5 NIV -- The plans of the diligent lead to profit as surely as haste leads to poverty.*

Utilize What You Have

The virtuous woman described in Proverbs had a sewing business. Out of her profits, she invested in real estate. You may have a talent that people are willing to pay for that will fund your passion. Build your network; some people may freely give you what you need. Do not forget the barter system. You can trade your time, talent and resources. Be creative! When you have your vision and mission clearly defined you will gain support for your passion. The government, banks, foundations and venture capitalists all have money waiting to give to someone with a great vision, but they want to see your due diligence.

A young woman in our church is a pastry chef. She created the most wonderful cake! It was green! I'm not a big sweet eater, so when I like sweets you better believe it's really good. I just always told her that her green cake was going to make her wealthy. Well, after years of preparation, she met a group of venture capitalists and guess what – they have invested in her business, helped her to create the plan, and she is on her way to great wealth! The lesson here is simple: keep God first, properly prepare, utilize what you have and manage well!

Prosper In Your Actions

God desires for us to prosper in our actions. If you do not move forward in your actions, you will not prosper. You cannot depend on anyone else to motivate you to take action, you must motivate yourself. Simply make up in your mind to take action, and then go do it! Go out and find an opportunity. Don't just sit and wait for it to happen. Go and make it happen. Act now!

My Personal Prosperity Passion Plan
Think about it and write it down!

_____
_____
_____
_____
_____
_____
_____
_____
_____
_____
_____
_____
_____
_____
_____
_____
_____

- ✓ A-Action
- ✓ C-Consistency
- ✓ T-Timing
- ✓ I-Innovation
- ✓ O-Ownership
- ✓ N-NOW

Your Checklist For Change

- ✓ **A-Action:** The process or state of acting or of being active; something done or performed; an act, a deed.

- ✓ **C-Consistency:** Steadfast adherence to the same principles, course, form, etc. Agreement, harmony, or compatibility.

- ✓ **T-Timing:** The selecting of the best time or speed for doing something in order to achieve the desired or maximum result.

- ✓ **I-Innovation:** Something new or different introduced; the introduction of new things or methods.

- ✓ **O-Ownership:** The state or fact of being an owner; legal right of possession.

- ✓ **N-NOW:** At the present time or moment; without further delay; immediately; at once.

TAKE ACTION NOW!

Chapter 6

Ignite Your Passion!

It only takes a spark to get
the fire glowing

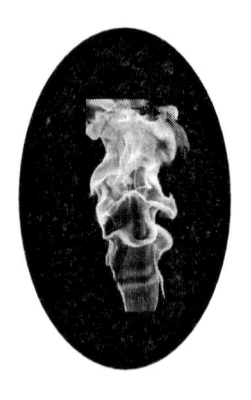

Ready, Set, Action!

You have been getting ready. Now you are set and it is time to run! What is your action plan? What are you willing to do in order to move forward in God – to finish the course? Everyday do something to fuel the flames of your passion. Everything that you need to live an incredible life already exists within you! The power is within, if you choose to use it!! *2 Peter 1:3 NIV, "His divine power has given us everything we need for life and godliness through our knowledge of him who called us by his own glory and goodness."*

So if you already have everything you need, then what's next? You must take action!

Action starts with setting clear, concise, doable goals. And once you set them, you have to take the steps to do them. A lot of people set goals, but few actually do them. A goal is a planned event, the result or achievement toward which <u>effort</u> is directed. It is an ongoing pursuit of a worthy objective until accomplished. Goal setting is the <u>beginning step</u> toward reaching your dreams. Dreaming is imagining or visualizing some things or some conditions that do not exist now, but one you would like to exist. Goal setting is getting specific with dreams – bringing them into a format where you can begin to work toward them and ultimately reach them.

There will be hurdles and obstacles, but the pursuit will be worth it when the reward is obtained.

---

*Philippians 2:16 NIV "... as you hold out the word of life-in order that I may boast on the day of Christ that **I did not run or labor for nothing.**"*

Set yourself on a specific path to succeed. There will be hurdles and obstacles, but the pursuit will be worth it when the reward is obtained. Your goals should be meaningful, specific and measurable. Setting and achieving goals is one to the best ways to measure your progress. Set S.M.A.R.T.E.R goals that will elevate you above the others to achieve your success.

S – Specific goals. Specific goals focus your energy and attention on what you need to do to achieve the goal. For example, "I want to lose weight or get fit" is an unclear goal and could be transformed into a more specific goal such as "I will lose 5 pounds" or "I will run 3 times a week".

M – Measurable goals. If you can measure your goals then you know how you are doing in your goal setting plan. An unclear goal such as "I want achieve financial independence" is hard to measure – so you won't know when you have achieved it. This goal could be transformed into a more measurable goal such as "I want to be debt free and have a passive income of $50,000 within 5 years".

A – Action-orientated. Having clear action steps to achieve your goal is important for goal setting success. What do you need to achieve your goals? For example, "I want more quality time with my family" may involve action steps such as; giving God for the first ten minutes of your day so that you can get clear; managing distractions at work, developing time management skills, and so forth, so that you can stop working overtime. Alternatively, it might involve watching less TV and doing more activities that actively involve the family.

R – Realistic. Setting realistic goals is important for your confidence and motivation. For example, if you have never run in your life, then setting a goal to run a marathon at the end of next month is setting yourself up for failure.

T – Time-based. Setting goals with time limits gives your goals a deadline. Deadlines raise the priority of something that needs to be done. Creating this sense of urgency, whether the goal is for today, next week, or next year, makes the goal a priority in your life. For example, "I want to get a degree" has no time lines, but if you put a time limit on this "I want to get a degree by next year," then this can create a sense of urgency and priority that motivates you towards action.

E – Energizing and Exciting. Your goals should be something that you are passionate about it. Passion gives you the motivation to keep going when things are tough, and there will be times when it is hard to be motivated. So you must learn to keep yourself energized by finding the excitement in what you are passionate about.

R – Rewarding and Reviewable – When you achieve your set goal give yourself a reward. By rewarding yourself you reinforce yourself for future success. At the same time, your goals should be reviewable. Your life circumstances change and with it so may your goals. For example, often athletes who become injured, or business people whose priorities change, need to adjust their goals to their current circumstances.

> *I refuse to go through life aimlessly, hoping that someday the wealth transfer will fall into my lap.*

SMARTer goals will maximize your goal setting success. By building on SMART goals, you take small focused steps so that today's dream can become tomorrow's reality.

You Must Have A Desire to Win Your Pursuit

In a race everyone runs, but only one person gets first prize. **So run your race to win. To win the contest you must deny yourselves many things that would keep you from doing your best.** I live by the principal 'Pay now, play later". What this means is that if I put in the time now; on the back end, as I move into my passion and reap the rewards of prosperity, I can enjoy life! *"So I run straight to the* *goal with purpose in every step. I fight to win. I'm not just shadowboxing or playing around. Like an athlete, I punish my body, treating it roughly,* **training it to do what it should, not what it wants to.** <u>*Otherwise I fear that after enlisting others for the race, I myself might be declared unfit and ordered to stand aside.*</u>" 1 Corinthians 9:24-27 TLB

Have you ever heard of the story of *The Little Engine That Could?* He was always thinking he could. "I think I can. I think I can. I think I can," he would say. My personal philosophy is 'If it is going to be, then it's up to me.' You must believe in yourself. I refuse to go through life aimlessly, hoping that someday the wealth transfer will fall into my lap. Like *The Little Engine That Could*, I THINK I CAN! I must put action to my desire!

Through my personal experience and my studies, I have found the common characteristics that all passionate people have?

- They have a get-it-done at any cost attitude.
- They are willing to do the extra stuff.
- They are driven by excellence.
- They are strong finishers.

Passionate people recognize that their passion is something that has to be fought for. The prize at the end of the fight is worth the pressure during the fight. The challenges and obstacles you encounter in your life are the lessons that help you discover who you really are. Do not try to bypass this part of the process. The process is necessary for you to discover you own source of inner strength and faith.

You will naturally be challenged in life. Inevitably things will go wrong. How you respond to obstacles will determine your quality of life. Your obstacles can be family, friends, debt, health issues, unexpected life events or circumstances beyond your control. You can choose to let them hold you back or find creative ways to remove or go around them. *James 1:12 NIV, "Blessed is the man who perseveres under trial, because when he has stood the test, he will receive the crown of life that God has promised to those who love him."*

Dare to be Disciplined

In Colossians 2:18, Paul tells the Colossians to not get disqualified. Who gets disqualified? Athletes who fail to follow the rules, the people who are rebellious; those who give up will be ineligible and ultimately be disqualified. So no matter what happens, do not give up on things, and absolutely don't give up on the larger more critical assignments. Stay on course! Become a Master! Be Disciplined!

Paul compared the Christian life to a race, and he told us: "Run your race to win. To win the contest you must deny yourselves many things that would keep you from doing your best" (1 Corinthians 9:24-25 TLB). He then adds: "Like an athlete, I punish my body, treating it roughly, training it to do what it should, not what it wants to" (1 Corinthians 9:27 TLB). In order to fulfill our God-given purpose and potential, we must deny ourselves things that would hinder us or weigh us down. If we don't rule and reign over our fleshly passions, appetites, and desires, they will rule and reign over us--and they will keep us from experiencing the good plans that God has for our lives. The Bible says that God has given us a spirit of discipline and self-control (2 Timothy 1:7 AMP). So by the power of the Holy Spirit, we can overcome everything we need to, if we will just yield to His leadership on a constant basis.

Strength and energy is given to your passion when you discipline yourself physically and mentally.

Strength and energy is given to your passion when you discipline yourself physically and mentally. Without proper training you will not be able to persevere when problems come. **Training is needed, both mentally and physically.** Your life goal should be to become a mature, whole, disciplined person.

The following components should be in your passion-training program:

- ❖ **Coach** - Everyone needs someone to instruct him or her. *Find a coach!*

- ❖ **Discipline** - Training expected to produce a specific character or behavior. *Discipline yourself!*

- ❖ **Conditioning** - Preparing for a specific action; being physically fit. *Condition yourself!*

- ❖ **Obedience** - God honors obedience – not emotion. You must be able to see beyond your circumstances and reach the goal in which He has awaiting you. *Be obedient!*

- ❖ **Self-Mastery** - Strive for the mastery!!! Be temperate (practice self-restraint)! Be disciplined! Keep to yourself! Excellence is the starting point! *Master yourself!*

Do you have a "get-it-done-at-any-cost attitude"?

Are you willing to do the extra stuff?

Are you driven by excellence?

Are you a strong finisher?

Are you willing to be obedient?

To Ignite My Passion I will:

Find a coach (List your new life coaches):

_____
_____
_____
_____
_____
_____
_____
_____
_____
_____

Become more disciplined by:

_____
_____
_____
_____
_____
_____
_____
_____
_____
_____

Become more conditioned by:

_____
_____
_____
_____
_____
_____
_____
_____
_____
_____

Render unyielding obedience by:

_____
_____
_____
_____
_____
_____
_____
_____
_____
_____

Strive for excellence in all that I do by striving for self-mastery! I will master myself by:

_____
_____
_____
_____
_____
_____
_____
_____
_____
_____
_____

Chapter 7

Live Your Passion

Whenever you are passionate, you will be productive; when you are productive, you will be prosperous; when you are prosperous, you will provide for your purpose.

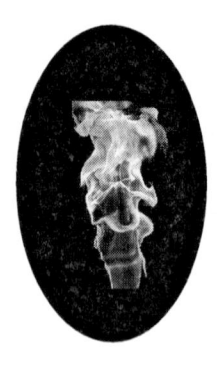

Be Committed

A person who is not passionately committed to the cause will draw little commitment from others. A passionate person understands that in order to be successful that you must be committed. True commitment inspires and attracts people. The world will liberally give to someone who knows what he or she wants, because there is not much competition when it comes to passionate commitment. Your organization will struggle if your actions are inconsistent with your words. If you are not committed to your cause, then others will not be either. Jesus' reaction to non-commitment: "It is better to be hot as fire or cold as ice, because if you are lukewarm I will spit you out."

Joseph was committed to excellence. In every situation he showed excellence, even in prison. Even the king noticed Joseph's commitment to excellence.

---

1 Corinthians 15:58 NIV, "Therefore, my dear brothers, stand firm. Let nothing move you. Always give yourselves fully to the work of the Lord, because you know that your labor in the Lord is not in vain."

The difference between average people and achieving people is their perception of and response to failure.

~John Maxwell

Passionate People:

- ❖ Nelson Mandela sat in jail over 20 years for his beliefs. The whole world saw his passion and commitment. He became president of the same nation that put him in jail.

- ❖ Elisha asked Elijah for a double portion of his spirit. He passionately served his spiritual father in spite of the ridicule from others around him. Elisha received what he asked for.

- ❖ Mother Teresa had a passion for the poor. Her passion inspired others to help her feed the hungry.

- ❖ Bill Gates had a passion to make computer operations simple for everyone. He dropped out of college to work his passion. He is now one of the richest men in the world.

Do you have a passionate commitment to a cause? If you do, be confident! If you do not believe it, neither will anyone else. Confidence is assurance; a state of mind marked by ease, coolness and freedom from uncertainty; reflecting self-control. When everyone says it cannot be done, you should ask, "How can it be done?" Dr. Robert H. Schuller told the world he was going to build a stunning Crystal Cathedral in California, at a cost of over twenty million dollars.

Although people laughed at his passion, he did it anyway. The Crystal Cathedral was dedicated debt-free at a cost just under thirty million dollars. Schuller commented, "I think when you have big dreams you attract other big dreamers." Several people donated more than a million dollars each to bring Schuller's passion to life.

1 John 5:14-15 NIV, "This is the confidence we have in approaching God: that if we ask anything according to his will, he hears us. And if we know that he hears us-whatever we ask-we know that we have what we asked of him."

The difference between you and those dreamers we told you about is that they were committed in their heart, and they had the confidence to take action! They also recognized that their commitment and passion pushed them passed any and all obstacles. In other words, their passion caused them to press on, and press through any and everything that attempted to cause them to fail. Always

> *Whether you are called to be a full-time mother, career person, business owner, coach, etc., if it is your passion, you will succeed.*

remember that God is on your side. He desires for you to step out of your box of complacency. God wants you to take the limits off of Him. God placed your passion in you, so that you would fulfill His purpose for you on the earth. In your passion, give it your best. Whether you are called to be a full-time mother, career person, business owner, coach, etc., if it is your passion, you will succeed. And you should perform that task with excellence! Mary, a spunky fifty-something year old friend of mine always says 'God gives you a life to live, why play dead! Live your life to the fullest!"

Every single day you live is another opportunity to share your passion with the world. The world needs you in your place doing your thing! Do it to the best of your ability! When God's purpose is fulfilled in you, He will be glorified through you. When you are in your passion, remember that your passion has POWER!

Conclusion

Final Thoughts

You can make a difference without compromising your own life goals.
~Stan Toler~

I hope that you have enjoyed reading this book as much as I have enjoyed writing it. However, I want you to understand that this book is intended as a tool to help you get a grip on your direction in life.

My prayer is that from reading **The Power of Passion** that you will discover who you are and what you are meant to do. This tool should be part of your process in planning how to pursue your passion.

If you are going to accomplish great things in life, then you must dream, plan, believe, and then act. I believe that if you integrate these components into your life, that you will be that much closer to igniting the power of your true inner passions. For it is in your passion, that your prosperity will come!

May you find success as you embark upon your own personal power toward your passions!

Passionate About EmPOWERment,

Dr. Renee Fowler Hornbuckle

Recipes for Success

Love what you're doing!
Believe in your product.
Select good People

~Debbie Fields
~Cookie Entrepreneur

Now, What Is Your Recipe For Success?

_____
_____
_____
_____
_____
_____
_____
_____

Let others lead small lives,

But not you.

Let others argue over small things,

But not you.

Let others cry over small hurts,

But not you.

Let others leave their future

In someone else's hands,

But not you.

~Jim Rohn

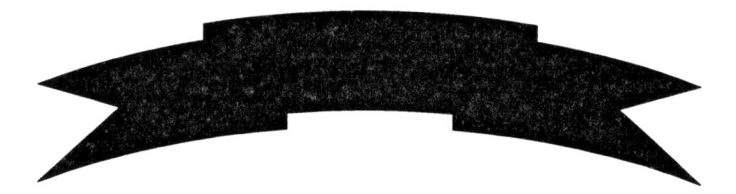

If you are going to accomplish great things in life, you must DREAM, PLAN, BELIEVE, and then ACT!

I believe that if you integrate these components into your life, you will be that much closer to IGNITING THE POWER of your true inner passions. FOR IT IS IN YOUR GOD-GIVEN PASSION, THAT YOUR TRUE PROSPERITY WILL COME!

~Renee Fowler Hornbuckle

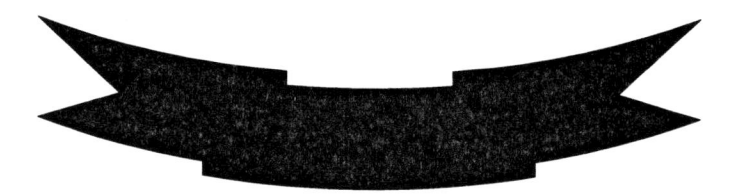

I will praise thee; for I am fearfully and wonderfully made: marvelous are thy works; and that my soul knoweth right well.

Psalms 139:14

POSSIBILITY PRAYER

Father, I thank You in the name of Jesus that You are the True and Living God. I bless Your name and I exalt Your Word. You are all powerful. You are Creator of all things and nothing that exits exists without You.

I commit my situation to You now knowing that though it seems impossible, Your Word declares that all things are possible with You. I cast all my cares upon You and trust that whatever I ask in the Name of Jesus, it shall be granted unto me. I will not be anxious or fretful about anything for I know that if You take care of the lilies of the field, You will take care of me. I am confident that no good things will You withhold from me and that Your plans are to prosper me and give me hope. I am certain that though there seems to be no way out, You always provide a way because You are the Waymaker. I will not allow despair and discouragement to overtake me for You are in control and I ask that Your perfect will be done. In Jesus' Name, Amen.

Matthew 6:26-32, 19:26; Jeremiah 29:11;
Philippians 4:6-7; I Peter 5:7

Copyright 2000 | Women of Influence, Inc.

Other Resource Tools By
Dr. Renee Fowler Hornbuckle

- ❖ The Power of Healthy Esteem
- ❖ Power For This Day
- ❖ Petals Principles & Promises
- ❖ The Power Journal
- ❖ If It Pleases the King

To order, please visit:
www.reneehornbuckle.org
or call 817.557.5811

BECOME A PARTNER TODAY!